The Good,
The Bad, and
The Complicated

Amy Grace

This is for you.
(and me)

Contents

Love

I fell in love.

The End

(and the beginning)

When I first saw you,

you looked like you were

going to ruin my life,

but all I could think was

perfect timing.

He smiled at me

and I knew I

was in trouble,

but in that moment

there was nowhere

else I wanted to

be than with him

right next to me.

"What? Why are you staring

at me?" she asked, as she smiled.

"You are the most interesting

person I have ever met, and you have

no idea how special you are."

You have some

kind of power

over me. I thought

I was strong, but

one look was all

it took, and I came

completely undone.

So, let's go there,

tell me everything.

I don't want to just

skim your surface;

I want to swim through

the depths of your sea.

I saw so much

of myself in him.

Everything I

shyly hid away,

he confidently

put on display.

Then suddenly,

everything lit up.

The sky,

your eyes,

my heart.

I didn't know

my heart had wings,

until you touched it

and it started to fly.

I love that

you don't talk

at me; you talk

to me, and you

don't just look

at me; you see

through me.

All you did was

hold my hand

and I knew you

would soon be

holding my heart.

Every time

I look at you,

I can see all

of the memories

we haven't yet

made together.

He pushed

my buttons

but they were

all the

right ones.

There is nothing

more attractive

to me than your

ability to seduce

me with your mind.

I was trapped inside,

and it was getting hard

to breathe, but you were

all the oxygen I needed.

Every time he

held me close,

I felt the fire

of his sweet embrace.

I'm stepping out

of my comfort zone

and running into

your arms.

He had fire

in his eyes,

and she lit up

every time he

looked at her.

If you want

to know what

it looks like

to be in love,

look at her

when she's

looking at him.

Falling in love

with him was like

falling into quicksand.

The harder I fought to

get out, the deeper I sank.

Our conversations

were endless,

except when we

were kissing,

but even then

they carried on

silently.

I was closed up in

my shell for so long

I forgot how to feel,

but you cracked me open

and just like that

a flood of emotions

came pouring out.

You can be whoever

you want to be with me,

but I really just want

you to be yourself.

I don't want perfect.

Perfect isn't real.

I want everything that

is real and everything

that is true.

I want you.

You must have opened

the eyes of my heart

because everything

became so clear

once I started feeling

things I've never felt.

"How do you know

if you are in love?"

If you don't know,

then you aren't.

I love your eyes

when they are looking at me.

I love your hands

when they are touching me.

I love your lips

when they are kissing me.

I love you, loving me.

When I look into your eyes,

I can see into your soul.

Everything you are hiding,

I already know. So, don't

be afraid to be yourself

with me. Just let go.

I thought you were

just going to be a chapter

in my story, but you became

the whole damn book.

I got lost in him,

but that is where

I found myself too.

My mind holds

many people,

my heart

holds some,

but my soul

only holds one.

I will never stop

wanting you as much

as I do now, even

when I have you.

You are

special because

I don't just love you;

I like you too.

I've loved a few

people before you,

but I didn't

like any of them.

I think I was

born to love you

because I have

never been better

at anything else.

You have

brought so

many things

out of me, but

my favorite

thing that

has come

out of me,

is me.

All the things

I hated about myself,

were all the things

I loved about you.

So, I guess when

I fell in love

with you, I fell in

love with myself too.

The moon,

wine,

and you.

-My favorite things

All my favorite

memories with you

come back to

me every time

I hear you laugh.

Open my mind

and you will

have a chance.

Touch my heart

and you will

be worth the fight.

Awaken my soul

and I'm yours

forever.

Your broken pieces

fit perfectly with mine.

That is why we feel whole

when we are together.

"You fill me," he said.

"I don't even know all of

the voids I had before you,

I just know that I don't

have them anymore."

If I could be anywhere

in the world right now,

I would be with you;

anywhere in the world.

I don't think

about anything

when I'm with you;

I just feel, and

I can't even tell

you how good it

feels to not think.

"Your words

are powerful."

No, my love for

you is powerful

because that is

where my words

come from.

Lack of Love

It was the lack of love

between us that pushed

me out the door first.

He just happened to be

on my front doorstep

as I was walking out.

"What happened?" It went like this. I found a house
that was nice and looked safe. I thought I could really
have a good life in this house, so I bought it, but the
only problem was there was a gate around the whole
house, so I could never actually get inside. I tried for
years to get through it even during the worst storms,
until I got really cold and tired, and I didn't have
the energy to try anymore so I gave up. That's when
I noticed another house right in front of me with no
gate and the door was wide open. I could see there
was a fireplace on inside and I had been cold and tired
for so long, so I went inside. Do you get it now?

Love should never

make you feel lonely.

It should fill up

every place inside

that's been torn apart,

so that loneliness

never has room to

enter your heart.

"I'm sorry," she said,

as she put her head in

her hands and started to cry.

"I love you, but I'm not

in love with you."

We were hanging by a thread

from the very beginning.

We should have known the

thread would eventually break.

Show her you love her

and make her feel loved

and she will give you

everything she has;

do the opposite

and she will have

nothing to give.

How am I supposed

to go back and try

after I have been gone

for so long? "You've only

been gone a few months."

Not physically gone;

emotionally gone.

Love shouldn't

be draining.

It should

fill you up;

not suck the

life out of you.

We have spent more time

trying to love each other,

than we have actually loving

each other and more time

trying to be what the other

person wants, than we have

actually being ourselves,

and it's getting exhausting.

I know I can say

some pretty hurtful

things sometimes but

I can promise you that

the things you don't say

hurt just as much.

-Silence is deadly

"Are you crying in the closet again?"

Yes. "Please stop doing that."

I just feel really low right now.

He is a good man and, regardless of

how he did or didn't make me feel,

he didn't deserve any of this.

"You didn't get to where you're at by

yourself though, and you are both good people.

Maybe you just aren't good for each other."

It just feels like we

are going nowhere fast,

and I am getting really

tired of running in place.

"I was never enough for you."

You're right, and I was always

too much for you.

You have to know

that it wouldn't be

fair to either of

us if I stayed.

We both deserve

a love that neither

of us are capable of

giving each other.

"You guys need to go to counseling

to work through your issues."

Does counseling make you

fall in love with someone?

We don't just have a

lack of communication.

We have a lack of love,

and that is the real issue

because it's the source of

all our other issues.

I have fought

with myself

for you

for so long.

-I surrender

The Good Kind
of Crazy

Yeah, he's a little crazy,

but he's the good kind of

crazy. The kind of crazy that

makes you want to be crazy too.

He is unlike

anyone I have

ever met because

he is everyone

I have ever met

in one person.

He made crazy

look romantic,

and I was

a hopeless

romantic.

He was like a

colorful abstract

painting that made

absolutely no sense,

but I was in love

with it, and I knew

I had to have it.

His energy

was so intense,

it made everyone

uncomfortable,

yet excited.

He is complicated,

but in a way

that makes perfect

sense to me.

He didn't whisper

sweet nothings;

he screamed his

intentions

loud and clear.

His mind was a

little all over

the place sometimes

but, wherever it went,

it was never boring.

He is either

his own worst enemy

or his number one fan.

There is no in-between.

Maybe he

was too much

sometimes,

but I couldn't

get enough.

The Mess

I did find

the beauty

in this mess.

I found you,

and that was

the best and

worst discovery

of my life.

I just can't pretend

that it didn't happen.

I've never been good at

pretending anyway.

It did happen,

and it changed

everything,

but most of all

it changed me.

They said you were fire

and not to get too close

because I might get burned,

but I wasn't afraid of getting

burned because I was cold,

and I needed your warmth

before I froze to death.

The most free

I have ever felt,

was when I was

hiding from the

world with you.

They said we were

living in a fantasy,

and maybe we were,

but I felt more alive

living in a fantasy

with you than I ever

have living in reality

with anyone else.

I'm not delusional.

I'm in love.

It just looks the

same sometimes.

This love is scary

because it's everything

I ever wanted

and, for some reason,

I'm scared of

everything I want.

"You," he said,

"will either be

the death of me,

or the life of me,

and I pray you are

the life because

I have been way

too close to death

too many times."

I am addicted to you

like a drug addict

who needs rehab.

The only problem is,

you are my rehab too.

I believe in you,

and I believe in us.

All you have to

do is believe too,

and that will be enough.

"I don't understand," she prayed.

"Why did this happen?

I didn't choose to fall

in love with him.

I can't help how I feel.

I want to do the right thing

but I want to be happy too.

Is it possible to have both?"

I'm happy because

I've never felt this way before,

and I'm sad because

I've never felt this way before.

I don't know what's

going to happen.

Truth is, I'm not

really sure about

anything, except

for the way I

feel about you.

"We have three options:

Stay and settle,

leave and deal

with the consequences,

or I'll shoot you

and you shoot me."

I think I like the

third option the best.

"Can I tell you a secret?

God already knows what

you are doing, so why

are you hiding from him?"

I feel like I'm dying.

"It's going to be okay."

Things are not okay for

anyone right now.

"But, they will be.

We will get through

this and it will

all work out."

I'm not so sure

about that anymore.

"I have to let you go now,"

she said, as tears filled her eyes.

She was instantly overwhelmed with

sadness, but she didn't know if it

was because she had to let him go

or because she knew she couldn't.

What are you doing here?!

You can't just show up here like this!

"You can't just shut me out like you did!"

We need to stay with them.

"So, you are going to decide that for me?"

It's for the best.

"For who? Everyone but us, right?

Look at me, this is not how it ends."

-Can't let go

I don't know what is worse,

feeling everything

or nothing at all.

You are either

heavy and consumed

or empty and unfulfilled.

I don't know what is

going on anymore

or what to believe!

We are both all over

the place and I can't

take it anymore!

I want off this

emotional rollercoaster!

Just when I thought I had enough

and I couldn't take anymore;

I took more, and I kept on taking

because, as much as the chaos

drove me mad, it was the only

thing that gave me any drive at all.

He said, "I'm sorry,

I'm just so mixed up right now.

I don't know what the right

thing to do is anymore because

I'm such a mess inside."

I loved you

with the best of

me when I held you

at your worst

because I was

at my worst too,

but I hid it so

that I could be

strong for you.

I don't care about

the mess that's

in your heart.

I just want

to be the one

holding you when

you fall apart.

Please stop telling me

that I deserve better.

I deserve you at your best,

and that is what you will be

when you are with me.

There is a truth

in your eyes that

words cannot hide.

So, when you tell

me you're okay,

I look at your eyes

to see what they say.

-Sad eyes

He said,

"I have never smiled

or cried as much

as I have with you."

It scared her how much

she was in love with him

because he had all the power.

He had the ability to

hurt her more than she

had ever been hurt,

but he also had the ability to

love her more than she

had ever been loved,

and that, to her,

was worth the risk.

I wish everyone

would just calm down!

It's not like we are

going to do anything crazy.

"We might."

What are we doing? Look at us!

We are laying on the cold hard

floor in an empty house

so that we can be together.

We are a hot mess right now!

"At least we are hot."

This isn't funny!

"Okay, sorry. Can we just

love each other tonight and

deal with our mess tomorrow?"

Okay.

"How is this going to work?

We are both crazy!"

Wrong. You are crazy.

I'm just complicated.

We are so close,

yet so far away,

and I think that is

the most frustrating

part about all of this,

always wondering what

day is going to be

"Someday".

I'm so tired of this back and forth!

Why can't we make up our minds?!

"Because it's not that simple,

and we are not that simple."

-Story of my life.

What do I do?

"You have to do the right thing."

But, what if "the right thing"

isn't the right thing for me.

"I miss you so much," she said,

as she laid her head on his chest.

"I'm right here," he replied.

"I know, but you won't be for long.

I can feel it in my heart.

So, I will miss you now, and

every day after you are gone."

I give up! I can't do this anymore. I can't breathe. I think I'm having a panic attack. I don't want to feel like this anymore. I just want it all to go away. Just make it go away. I am sorry to everyone for everything. I give up. "You are not giving up! Do you know how many times I wanted to give up through this whole mess?! I read this verse this morning. Galatians 6:9: "Let us not become weary in doing good for at the proper time we will reap a Harvest if we do not give up." "Do not let the enemy win."

-Breaking point

I tried to save you

when you started to drown,

but all you did was

pull me down with you, so

I had to let go

to save myself.

Now I get why they say,

"Be careful what you wish for."

My whole life I wished for

the kind of love that I found

but, once I got it, it

also came with a lot

of pain, utter chaos,

and complete destruction.

I love you

and you love me,

what a sad

love story

that will never be.

I did what I was

supposed to do and

crawled back into my

shell, trying to forget

everything that happened

and deny everything I felt.

Trying to forget you

is like trying to

forget my name.

"I miss you."

I miss you too.

"I just wanted

to tell you that

I'm sorry for

everything."

Me too.

I hate that the only

way I can see you,

is when I close my eyes.

I swim through

thoughts of

you and I

every day,

but tonight

I am drowning

in the memories.

I am going through with the divorce. "Are you sure?"
Yes. This is the hardest decision I have ever had to make
in my life. I've been struggling with it a lot but, since
I've been back, I've tried to get there with him, but we
are further apart than ever and so much damage has
been done. We were already hanging by a thread before
any of this happened, you know? "Yeah, counseling
didn't help?" No. There is only so much a counselor
can do if your heart isn't in it. I don't want this to
affect what you do because this is a decision I know I
need to make for myself regardless of what you do. I
just wanted to tell you because we said we would.

"I still feel

like you are mine."

I am, and I always

will be, whether I

want to be, or not.

I think I have always been

a pretty smart person

but nothing has made me

more stupid than falling in love.

"So, that's what happens when

you fall in love? You just lose

all your brain cells?"

Yeah, pretty much.

-Stupid in love

Are you sure this is what you really want?

"Yes." Then, I need a commitment from you.

I can't do half in and half out anymore.

"What is your problem?" I don't feel like

you are being completely honest with me.

"I guess you don't really know me then."

I do know you, and that is my problem.

I think I have been

a little too understanding,

to the point where it's starting

to feel more like naïve.

"I'm worried about you." When aren't you? "I'm being serious. Going through your divorce was hard enough for you emotionally and I don't think you have even had a chance to fully process it or heal from it all because you have been so consumed with him. I just don't want to see you go through more heartbreak if things don't work out with him." I know, and I am going into this knowing that I might get hurt, but I would rather give it a try and get hurt than live with never knowing, because then I would never be able to move on. "I know, just be careful." You know me, I love to learn the hard way.

Falling in love with you

has been the craziest ride

of my life but, at some point,

this rollercoaster has to

come to an end.

I feel like you are losing interest

in me. "No, I'm not." (I just feel the

end coming, so I am detaching myself so it

doesn't hurt as bad when it happens.)

-This feels familiar

The End and The Beginning

Once you are over

the sadness of the end,

you find the happiness

of a new beginning.

Why?! Why wouldn't he let me go

a long time ago?!! All those times

I tried to end it and he wouldn't

let me and now this is how it ends?!

"It doesn't matter how it ended.

All that really matters is that

you begin again."

There are always going to be

ups and downs in life.

That's why we need to

surround ourselves with people

who are going to build us up

when we are down and distance

ourselves from people who

bring us down when we are up.

Well, everyone was right, I got too

close to the fire and got burned.

"I tried telling you he was the devil."

Stop. "Fine, but maybe next time you should

look for the sunlight in someone instead.

You need someone who makes you glow, not

someone who gives you third-degree burns."

-Like a moth drawn to a flame

Don't you dare believe

that this is the end of you.

The sun will rise again

tomorrow and, just like the sun,

you will rise too and do

what you were meant to do; shine.

-Rise and shine

I deserve this.

This is my karma

for everything I did.

"No, losing him is your

blessing, and you might not

see that now but one day

you will thank God for not

giving you what you wanted.

Losing you, on the other hand,

is his karma."

There can be purpose hidden

in even the deepest kind of pain,

but if you focus too much on the

hurt, you will never see the gain.

I just want to be fully loved and fully chosen. One chose me but didn't know how to love me, and one loved me but didn't know how to choose me. "Sweetheart, you are fully loved and fully chosen by the God of the Universe and, once you learn to accept that love and love yourself too, you will never search for your worth in another man again."

-Chosen and loved

Don't be afraid of pain.

I know it hurts now,

but after it's done

breaking you down,

it builds you up,

and you always come

out better and stronger.

I feel like a failure. "You are not a failure, and God's grace is bigger than any mistake you could ever make. What verse did you get tattooed on your back when you were eighteen?" 2 Corinthians 12:9. "Remember that verse every time you mess up because you will again."

-Amazing Grace

Anything that takes

a great amount of

courage, will usually

require the same amount

of patience.

I'm tired of learning lessons.

Can I get blessings now?

"As long as you are making mistakes,

you are going to keep getting lessons,

but the good thing is, the blessings

are what come from the lessons."

-Lessons and blessings

Today is our Anniversary.

"I know, are you okay?" Yeah, just sad.

I cried all day. "I'm sorry, do you miss him?"

I don't know, I think it's mostly the memories,

you know? Endings are always sad but sometimes

it's not even so much the person that you miss.

It's the years, the routine, and the memories.

Every time I thought I couldn't,

I did because I had to.

-Responsibility

I don't like this.

This doesn't feel like my house,

and it's giving me anxiety.

It feels weird. I want

to go back to my house.

"Calm down, it's okay.

It's going to feel weird

for a little while, but it

will get better in time.

I promise."

-Change is hard

Sometimes being strong

has more to do with

how you handle what you have

and less to do with

what you have to handle.

Am I too old to get adopted?

"Stop it! You can do this."

How? I have nothing. He's

right, I don't know what I'm doing.

I am literally starting over with

no money and no plan. Tell me how am

I going to do this? My kids deserve

better than what I can give them on

my own. "Your kids deserve a mother who

is happy. You will figure it out

like you always do. You are the

strongest person I know and

you were made to save yourself."

-You got this

There will be some people you
meet in your life who will know
you before they even know anything about
you, and then there will be some people
who know everything about you, but
really don't know you at all. Hold on to
the ones who truly know who you are
and not just what you have done.

"Are you okay?" Yeah, I'm great! Why? "You don't sound great." I was just thinking. "That's scary. About what?" About how much I hate people. "Oh Lord, here we go." Especially guys! I really hate guys. They should just go to their own guy planet and be stupid together. "Are you drinking wine?" Maybe. "How much have you had to drink?" A glass. "A glass?" A glass bottle. "Oh my God, put the bottle down." I did, it went down very well. I don't hate all people... I love my people, you know? Like you. You are my person, but guys are still stupid. "I know, I think you should go to bed now." Okay, love you. "Love you too."

-Because people

Is there a way to change your relationship status
on Facebook to "Single and not ready to mingle"
or "I want to be alone forever?" Maybe I could just
change my name to "My name is no" then they
will leave me alone, right? "Probably not."

"Wow, you are the

most beautiful woman

I have ever seen,

and he is such a fool."

"Why are you laughing?" Because I can't believe my life right now. "Why? Oh my God, did you meet someone?!" Yep, and I don't even know how to explain this one… it's complicated. "I can only imagine. I thought you hated guys and wanted to be alone forever?" Yeah, that was the plan. "So, what happened?" Shots happened. "Oh no." Oh yeah. I'm going to just crawl into a hole and die. "It was that bad?" I don't remember, but I was told we put on a good show for everyone. "It's okay, we have all been there." Yeah, but that's not really where I wanted to go after everything that's happened. "You know what, I'm not even mad at you. Anything that gets your mind off what's-his-face, I am all for! Besides, you like him, right?" Apparently. My life is like a really bad Lifetime movie. "Or, a really good one! I can't wait to see what happens next!" Yeah, me neither! Life just keeps surprising me.

-Shots happen

"You are like

nothing I've ever had

and everything

I've always wanted."

"You do realize that you now have feelings for three people at the same time, right?" Yep, stupid shots. "You can't blame it all on the shots. I know he's a good guy but he's also a distraction and you know it. You haven't given yourself any time to really deal with your feelings and to get over them. You have just gone from one person to the next and that's why you are so confused. Being with someone else might help take your mind off of things, but it doesn't take the feelings away or the hurt you still have deep inside. Your heart needs time to heal those wounds. I will always love them though, so why does it matter? "Maybe you will, and that's okay but, if it still hurts when you think about them, that means you haven't dealt with what you need to, so you are just going to be giving that to someone else to deal with too." I hate this, you know. I never in a million years thought I would be in this position. Growing up, I thought love was simple. Either you love someone, or you don't, but it's not that simple and love isn't the same with every person. My ex-husband was the first real "grown up" love that I experienced but it wasn't like fireworks. It was comfortable and safe. I thought that was the kind of love you build a life with, but I still always felt like something was missing. Then, the other kind of love was like fireworks. It was passionate but dangerous too. It was the kind of love that made you crazy in good ways and in bad ways. And, I don't even know what this new one is yet. I'm just going with it, except I don't really know where it's going.

-Fifty shades of love

"I feel like you want me

to be messed up or something."

No, not exactly.

"What does that mean?"

Well, I mean I want deep,

but not a psychopath.

"I'm not a psychopath."

That's a start.

I have to tell you something.

"What?" I'm really complicated.

"You say that like you are telling

me you have a disease or something."

It feels like that sometimes.

Thank you, God, for loving me

when I have a hard time

loving myself and for

never giving up on me

when I want to

give up on myself.

I'm sorry I'm so emotional. I really have been doing good lately and thought I was over everything, but I guess I'm not. "It's okay, I wouldn't expect you to be over everything so soon, and I want to help you through this, but I can't help you with that part. All that guilt and shame that you are holding onto, you have to give to God and forgive yourself. You aren't doing anything wrong anymore. It's okay to be happy now."

-Forgive yourself

I didn't know where

I was going,

until I got lost.

Just because you miss someone,

doesn't always mean you want

to be back with them,

and just because you still

love someone, doesn't always mean

you haven't moved on either.

There are

some things

I have to do

for myself,

by myself.

Once you remember

who you are,

you will forget

who he was.

I just realized

for the first time

this morning that

I didn't wake up

thinking about him.

If it doesn't bring me more

comfort than my favorite

blanket and a cup of coffee

on a rainy day then,

I don't want it.

-Solitude

I needed this. "Needed what?"

To be alone for a while

to figure out what makes me

happy on my own so that I never

put my happiness in someone

else's hands again.

 -Whole on my own

I know everything happened for a reason,

but I was wrong about what the reason was.

I used to think it was for us or maybe just him,

but now I know it was for me.

-Seasons and reasons

"I am so happy you are

in a better place now."

Me too. You were right,

and he was right.

"About what?"

That I deserve better.

As much as I love him,

I love myself more.

He made the right choice.

You know all

those things

you tell yourself

you can't do?

Do them!

"What's your plan?"

To right all my wrongs.

"How are you going

to do that?"

The only way I know how;

write a book and

maybe a few songs.

"I want to talk to you about your purpose. Purpose starts with the gifts we are given. Do you know what your gift is?" Writing? "No, it's more than just writing. There are a lot of people who like to write and are good at it, but what is the point if you don't have anything good to write about. Your gift is your words and your purpose is how you use them, and isn't it amazing that all you have to do to fulfill your purpose is use your words."

-Purpose

Maybe it's not about

the happy ending for me.

Maybe it's about the story,

and that's okay because

I'm happy with the story.

Perfectly
Imperfect

She was perfectly imperfect,

and that's what made her beautiful

because she didn't hide her scars;

she wore them like jewelry.

It's just so exhausting. "What is?" Trying to be perfect all the time. It's like the more I try to do everything perfectly, the more I mess up and the harder I am on myself. It's just an exhausting cycle you know? I mean, why do we all put ourselves in this prison of perfectionism?! Everyone is afraid to be real because real is messy, but kids are messy and look how happy they are! You don't see them crying over spilled milk. They mess up and forget about it in two minutes, but we mess up and beat ourselves up about it for the rest of our lives. We all just need to be a little more like kids. Messy, happy, and free.

-Be messy

All she wanted was

someone who understood

the deepest parts of her

and who could make sense

of the beautiful mess

inside of her.

What you see is not

what you get with me.

I am so much more than I

will ever let anyone see.

"You are everything," he said,

"and when you are everything,

you can be anything."

She was strong like whiskey

and soft like wine.

Her heart is an open book

to those who can read it.

It is written in a

language few understand.

"So, what are you good at?"

Figuring people out,

talking to myself,

daydreaming,

overthinking,

hiding from people.

You?

Her heart is a work of art.

Don't mess up something so

beautiful by tearing it apart.

She will give you

advice like a best friend,

support you like a sister,

defend you like a brother,

comfort you like a mother,

protect you like a father,

and love you like a lover.

So, don't say you don't have

anyone. If you have her, you have

everyone you will ever need.

She didn't

want anyone

to worship

the ground

she walked on;

she just wanted

someone to

walk with her.

Darling,

Don't get lost

in the madness;

be the madness

and everything else

will get lost.

She was a walking contradiction.

She was strong, yet fragile.

A lover and a fighter.

Private, but she wore her heart

on her sleeve, and she knew exactly

what she wanted, but was entirely

indecisive at the same time.

She was predictable at being

unpredictable, and she didn't

expect anyone to understand

her because she didn't even

understand herself at times.

If you could swim

through the depths

of her mind, you would

probably drown.

She had a

beautiful way

of turning chaos

into poetry

and madness

into a masterpiece.

I'm not alone.

I'm never alone.

I have my thoughts

and a sky full of stars

to keep me company.

And sometimes,

I will feel like

I have to run

but don't worry,

I won't leave.

I just drift

from time to time,

but I will never go

too far from where

I'm meant to be.

-The dreamer in me

She is hardheaded

but softhearted.

Telling me you believe me

is like a nice pat on the back,

but telling me you believe in me

is like giving me a nice pair

of wings to help me fly.

She believed she would

make all her dreams come

true, but if you believe

in her, she will make all

of your dreams come true too.

Country kind of heart,

R & B kind of soul.

She had an overwhelming

sense of purpose, she just

didn't have a good sense of direction.

She didn't know where she was going,

but she knew she would get there.

She turned

her problems

into poetry

and solved

them all.

The Struggle

It's a never-ending battle

when you are at war with yourself.

She was at war with

herself all the time.

Her religious side fought

with her spiritual side.

Her logical side fought

with her intuitive side.

Her realist side fought

with her idealist side.

Her practical side fought

with her dreamer side.

Her reserved side fought

with her outgoing side.

This was her struggle

because she was never

one or the other.

She was both at

the same time.

"What do you mean you don't fit in?

You fit in everywhere!"

I know, that's the problem.

I fit in a little everywhere

but never fully anywhere.

That is why I feel like I can

understand everyone a little but no

one will ever fully understand me.

You know, it's funny... I have spent my entire life trying to find myself, going through so many different stages, and making so many mistakes just trying to figure out which version of myself was really me, until I finally realized that they are all me. Growing up, everyone else seemed to know their place and had their group, but I never really knew where I belonged. I mean, I chose one main group, but I would still look at other people and think, okay, I'm like her, but I'm like her too and her, and him. I looked like an outgoing cheerleader on the outside, acted like a shy awkward nerd, and felt like a gothic misfit on the inside. I would gravitate toward the outcasts sometimes, even though I never talked to them, I wanted to. I wanted to say, I know we look different on the outside, but I bet we feel the same on the inside.

-Multidimensional

When you see both
sides to everything,
you are always stuck
in the middle.

My mind is a cage

and I am a bird trapped inside.

I wonder if it will ever

let me out, so I can fly.

"There is nothing wrong with you,"

the counselor said. "You are able to

see things from a perspective a lot

of people don't. You are different."

I know, but is that like a good

different, or a bad different?

No one knew the battle she

fought inside of her every day,

but no matter how dark it got,

she kept her smile and shined

her light for anyone who needed

it, even though she knew she was

the one who needed it the most.

Do you want to hang out this weekend?

"Sure, but I can't go out of town or

drive because my anxiety has been really

bad lately." Well, I have anxiety about

staying in town because I don't want to

see or talk to anyone I know.

"Sushi at my house?"

Perfect!

-Anxiety problems

I don't know what

I am more afraid of,

living in the unknown

or dying in the familiar.

I think most women go through a little bit of an identity crisis when they are in their thirties, no matter what stage of life they are in. If you are married with kids, you focus on being a good mother and a good wife but, at some point, you start to feel like you are losing yourself in those roles, so you look for outlets and things you can do to help you feel like yourself again and give you some sort of purpose other than being a mom and a wife. If you are single, you start to get discouraged that you won't find anyone to settle down with and, if you haven't had kids by now, the fear of the clock running out before it's too late really sets in. If you don't have a solid job or career, you feel like you should go to school or start something new, otherwise you will feel like you aren't living up to your full potential or that you haven't accomplished anything in everyone else's eyes. Then, at some point, you will feel like you have to do all of the things you always said you would do because you spent your twenties doing all of the things you said you wouldn't do. Then, suddenly it hits you that you are getting older and you need to reconnect with your friends again since you also spent the second half of your twenties growing up and distancing yourself from friends. You start to realize how important it is to have a support system or at least someone to vent to over coffee or wine and see if someone else feels the same way you do and that you are not going crazy.

I think we all question where we are at in our thirties;
if we are truly happy and, if we aren't, then why aren't
we? So, anxiety comes up out of nowhere, or gets worse.
Then, probably the biggest struggle about being in your
thirties is your young side fighting with your old side.
It's like some days you still feel like you are twenty and
you are taking selfies on Snapchat and Instagram using
hashtags like #yolo and #nofilter (even though it is a
filter, just not the one with bunny or kitty ears) and
rapping in the car on the way to the gym, rocking your
new tank that says, "Drop it like a squat." Then, other
days, you are in your PJs all day pinning recipes on
Pinterest and thinking about how you should redecorate
your living room or if you should learn how to knit a
scarf. Being in your thirties is a confusing time, and
everyone's paths might look a little different, but most
of us need the same things; a few good friends, girls'
nights, alone time, pizza to be healthy, to be young every
once in a while, to be old every once in a while, to say
no and not feel guilty, to say yes and not feel selfish,
something for ourselves, appreciation, encouragement,
support, vacations, coffee, wine, counseling, and Xanax.

-Thirty-something

I have a hard time

doing anything that

my heart isn't into.

If I don't love it,

it's a struggle,

but if I do love it,

I love it with a passion.

Do you think there are brother-husbands? "Brother what?"
You know, like sister-wives? How come we never hear
about brother-husbands? I mean really, who needs five
wives?! One is more than enough, but five husbands, on
the other hand, is different. "How do you even come up
with this stuff?" Well, think about it. Most women are
already like five people in one. We do it all. You know
that song, "I'm every woman, it's all in me"? "Yeah!"
See, Whitney knew what was up, but it's rare to find the
same in a man, and women need more from men than
men need from women. Let's see, we need the strong,
stable, responsible, trustworthy, and reliable one who
will never let you down. The handy man who can fix
anything and help you with your Pinterest projects, and
who also cooks and cleans would be a plus, the hot one
who makes your heart race and meets physical needs.
The deep, passionate, comforting, encouraging, and
supportive one who listens to you intently, is loving,
affectionate, and meets all your emotional needs. Then,
finally, the best friend one that you can be yourself with,
have fun with, laugh with, and talk to about anything.
"Oh my God, you are right, we do need brother-husbands.
How do we find them?" There's got to be a website
like brotherhusbandsonly.com, right?" Nowadays, I
wouldn't doubt it. You do know that I'm joking, right?
"I'm really interested now." I can't stop laughing.

-Iso brother-husbands

She felt invisible,

not because people

didn't notice her,

but because she couldn't

reveal what was in her heart.

"Do you want to know how to become more confident and love yourself more too?" How? "Stop looking at all those things that make you feel different as weird, and start looking at them as unique and special. Instead of thinking you are some sort of alien that no one will understand because you have so many different sides, start seeing yourself as a colorful unicorn that has a color everyone can relate to."

-Perspective

I have this old and wise soul

with a young and rebellious heart

that gets me into trouble sometimes.

"So, when do you think the social anxiety started?" the counselor asked. Probably around eight years old. That's when I started to feel like I was different from other kids. "Different how?" Like when everyone else was playing outside, I was inside staring out the window and wondering what the meaning of life was and what my purpose was. "That is called being an introvert and having an old soul. I bet that felt weird for you." It did. I felt like I had a deep understanding about people and life at a young age, but I didn't know how. I couldn't just think about what I was going to eat for dinner like every other kid. Instead, I daydreamed about how I could make a difference in the world without being noticed too much.

-Small girl in a big world

I can't say anything

when I feel too much,

and I can't feel anything

when I think too much,

but I don't know how

to not do either.

I can't believe we are in our thirties. "I know, I still feel like we are sixteen sometimes." Me too. Do you ever feel like you don't know what you are doing with your life? You know, like the days pass by but nothing changes, and you are just going through life on autopilot? "Yeah, I feel like that every day. Sometimes I don't even know where I'm at." What do you mean? Like when you get anxiety? "Yes." Oh, okay. Do you think people would think we are weird if they heard what we talked about? "Probably, but I don't care, at least we are funny." But, are we really funny? Or, are we just funny to each other? "Does it really matter?" No, but, for the record, I think we are hilarious.

-God made us best friends

Everything is heavy

when you have a

complicated mind

and a deep soul.

You go there;

you go everywhere.

I'm always in my own head.

No matter where I am at,

or what I am doing,

I can't get out of my head.

It's like I am here,

but I'm not really here.

How do I learn how to really be here?

"You have to be somewhere

you would rather be at more

than in your own head."

It's usually the things

you never see coming that

open your eyes to the things

you couldn't see before.

I discovered something lifechanging today.

"Really? What?!!" I'm an INFJ! "What's that?"

It's the rarest personality type of the Myers-Briggs

sixteen personality types. Only 1% of the population

is INJF, and it explained so much for me! I literally

felt like everything I've struggled with my entire life

finally made sense when I read about the INFJ.

"Like what kind of things?" Just like always feeling

misunderstood growing up, contradicting myself

all the time, or never knowing exactly where I fit

in, and even the social anxiety part! All of it!

-INFJ

The Truth

Speak your truth,

and walk in freedom.

A closed mind will never understand an open heart. That is why so many people hold their own hearts hostage because they don't want to trust something that they don't understand.

Take a chance.

I promise you,

the what-if's

will kill you

more than the

shouldn't-haves.

I have never met

a happy person

who did everything

right.

I get it; logical makes sense.

That is why so many of us go

with the logical choice.

That is also why so many of us

don't go anywhere at all.

People want to open up

but, the problem is,

everyone is waiting

for someone else

to open up first.

Too many people

are living life

dying inside

because they are

too afraid to

talk about the

things they hide.

Don't worry about what

people say about you.

It's always the ones

who have the most to say

that are the ones who have

the most to hide too.

If you stop

lying to yourself,

you won't have to

lie to anyone else.

Some people love playing games

so much that they play forever,

all the while completely oblivious

to the fact that they never win

because they never lose either.

They remain stuck in their own game,

always playing but never winning.

-Play on playa

Why is it that the ones

who are just trying to

seek attention, make all

the connections, but the

ones who are genuinely

trying to make a connection,

don't get enough attention?

-The problem with society

The thing about me is,

when someone hurts me,

I know I can hurt them

back with what I know,

but I've never needed to

because they always end

up hurting themselves

in the end anyway.

I've been hurt,

and I've hurt

people too.

I'm no better,

or no worse

than you.

-Human

I'm not a hypocrite.

I am a Christian

and I am a sinner,

just like you.

-Saved by Grace

There is a stairway to Heaven,

but no one wants to take the stairs,

so instead, they jump on

the highway to Hell.

-Take your time on the climb

Don't be afraid of the stumbling blocks the Devil puts in your way. God can turn them into stepping stones if you just have faith.

-Faith>fear

You will eventually lose

faith, if you are always

believing in the wrong things.

Love will either kill you,

or make you stronger.

That all depends on

who you love.

Why do people have a harder time letting go of the things that are bad for them, rather than the things that are good for them? Exercise and eating healthy make you feel good, but drugs and alcohol do too. The only difference is, one hurts you and one helps you, yet people always seem to go back to the people or things that hurt them the most, even if they know that what's making them feel good is also killing them too.

-Bad habits

If someone tells you

that you deserve better,

believe them.

Just because someone is alone,

doesn't mean that they are lonely,

and just because someone is with

someone, doesn't mean they're not.

How do you know

when you have

found the one?

When you stop

looking.

Nothing will mess you up

more than your own feelings.

Good people do bad things

either because they want

to feel something, or

because they don't want

to feel anything at all.

-Because feelings

Be who you were when you were eight.

That is who you really are,

before life challenged you

and people changed you.

There is so much more

to life and people

than you think.

You just have to be

brave enough to knock

down the walls in your

own life and the walls

surrounding other people's

hearts. You will be glad

you did because there

is always more to be found.

-Layers

I don't know why it's such a

bad thing to need someone.

We were made to need other people.

You just have to need the right people.

The ones who make you feel like you

don't need them, even though you

know you do. Otherwise, it's dependency

and those are two different things.

.

"How do you know everything

is going to work out?"

Because I believe in real things,

real people, and real love.

You can "fake it til you make it"

but that's also how you will break it.

-Faith it til you make it

I don't have much money,

but I do have words,

and those are worth

a lot more.

You can give

life to your words,

if you let them exist

outside of your mind.

Speak your truth,

and then live

out your words.

There is no greater

freedom than that.

It's all just one big experiment, isn't it? It's just a lot of trial and error until eventually you've messed up just enough times to figure out what works and what doesn't and, even then, it doesn't always turn out the way you think it will but that's the beauty of it. Sometimes it turns out better, and sometimes our biggest mistakes lead us to our greatest discoveries.

-Life

The End

(and the beginning)

Instagram

@a.gracequotes

37584141R00146

Made in the USA
Middletown, DE
28 February 2019